I SPY PHONICS FUN

Learning Letters M and N

In this book you'll see letters printed in red. These are *I Spy Phonics Fun* learning letters. Learning the sounds of these letters will help you read.

The learning letter "m" sounds like the "m" in "monkey."

The learning letter "n" sounds like the "n" in "napkin."

I Spy Sight Words

You will see the following words in this book. The rhythm, rhyme, and repetition of the I Spy riddles will help you learn them.

I	spy	a
an	that	with
the	in	and

I Spy Challenge Words

When you come to these words, the I Spy pictures will help you remember them.

nose	flat	ear	balloon
little	pail	bat	person

I spy

a magnet,

 a man with a bat,

a pumpkin's smile,

 and a small flat hat.

I spy

a motorcycle,

 a nose on a moon,

a man with a cane,

 and a little balloon.

I spy

 a nickel,

a shiny red horn,

 the man in the moon,

and an ear of corn.

I spy

 a dragon,

a little nail,

a wooden N,

and a person with a pail.

I spy two words that start with the letter M.

match

kite

mask

I spy two words that start with the letter M.

marble

mouse

lipstick

I spy two words that start
with the letter N.

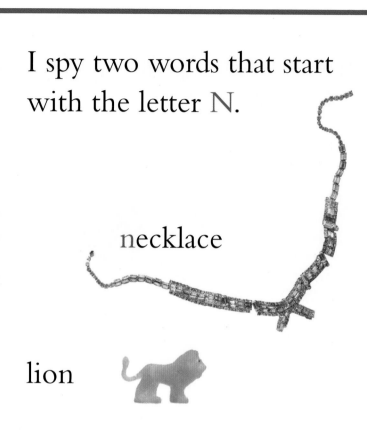

necklace

lion

nest

I spy two words that end with the letter N. Do they rhyme?

pan

kangaroo

van

I spy two words that have both an M and an N.

man

key

moon

I spy these M words
somewhere else in this book.

magnet

pumpkin's smile

motorcycle

I spy these N words somewhere else in this book.

nickel

horn

dragon

nail